Classical Themes

Favorite orchestral works arranged for piano solo
by Fred Kern, Phillip Keveren, and Mona Rejino

Text Author
Barbara Kreader

Editor
Margaret Otwell

Concepts introduced in *Classical Themes Level 1:*			
Classical Themes Level 1 is designed for use with the first book of any piano method. Some methods may label their first book as *Book 1* (such as the *Hal Leonard Student Piano Library*), and others may label their first book a *Primer*.	**Range**	**Symbols** *p, f, mp, mf*	**Keyboard Guides** show hand placement L.H. R.H. F G A B C D E 4 3 2 1 1 2 3
	Rhythm 4/4 time signature 3/4 time signature	**Intervals** 2nds, 3rds, 4ths	

To access audio visit:
www.halleonard.com/mylibrary

Enter Code
6854-5242-4079-1913

ISBN 978-1-4950-4761-9

HAL•LEONARD®
CORPORATION

7777 W. BLUEMOUND RD. P.O. BOX 13819 MILWAUKEE, WI 53213

In Australia Contact:
Hal Leonard Australia Pty. Ltd.
4 Lentara Court
Cheltenham, Victoria, 3192 Australia
Email: ausadmin@halleonard.com.au

Visit Hal Leonard Online at
www.halleonard.com

Table of Contents

About the Compositions

George Frideric Handel (1685-1759)

In the German composer George Frideric Handel's time, the suite was a popular musical form. Each suite contained several pieces of varying tempos, based on popular dance rhythms. This *Air* from Handel's *Water Music* suite was first performed during a royal procession down London's River Thames on barges in July of 1717. Imagine the sound of the original orchestra as you play. It included two oboes, one bassoon, two horns, strings, and a natural trumpet – one without valves.

Jacques Offenbach (1819-1880)

The *Can-Can* comes from the German/French composer Offenbach's comic operetta, *Orpheus in the Underworld*, a story that pokes fun at Greek myths. Orpheus, a violin teacher in Thebes, finds out that Pluton has carried Orpheus' wife, Euridice, to the underworld. Orpheus thinks Euridice has died, but a character named Public Opinion demands that Orpheus descend to the underworld and rescue her. Meanwhile, the gods do nothing to help. They merely sit around complaining about their boring diet of nectar and ambrosia.

Johann Strauss, Jr. (1825-1899)

The famous 19th-century German composer Johann Strauss was known as the "Waltz King." During Strauss' time, all of Europe enjoyed the new dance, the waltz. As the leading dance composer of his day, Strauss wrote waltzes so elegant and inspiring that people treated him with the same awe that we reserve for rock and pop music stars today. Strauss took the Viennese waltz to new heights, however, making it as popular in the concert hall as it was on the dance floor.

Edvard Grieg (1843-1907)

The Norwegian composer Edvard Grieg wrote this simple melody to accompany his countryman Henrik Ibsen's drama *Peer Gynt*. Ibsen's imaginative story takes the listener to such fantastic places as Arabian villages and lands where trolls live. *Morning* sets the mood for the opening of Act IV, which takes place in Africa. Peer and his friends enter, laughing and teasing one another. Grieg wrote about his inspiration for *Morning*: "I imagine the sun breaking through the clouds at the first *forte*."

The Nutcracker is the Russian composer Pyotr Il'yich Tchaikovsky's most famous ballet. Even today it is performed worldwide, especially at Christmas time. Clara, a young girl, falls asleep on Christmas Eve and dreams that her wooden nutcracker, a gift from a mysterious character named Drosselmeyer, comes to life as a prince. The Nutcracker Prince escorts her to his magical kingdom where his courtiers dance in her honor. When the Russian dancers hear *Trepak,* they leap and twirl around the stage with high energy, much to Clara's delight.

The German composer Ludwig van Beethoven composed nine symphonies. His *Third Symphony* became known as the *Eroica,* or Heroic Symphony. At first Beethoven dedicated the music to the famous French general, Napoleon. When he later discovered that this mighty military hero was more interested in conquering countries and proclaiming himself Emperor than in liberating the poor, Beethoven's famous temper flared. He angrily erased Napoleon's name from the title page. Despite this change of heart, the music retains a heroic mood.

For many years, people thought the British composer Henry Purcell wrote this popular music. Clarke, also from England, originally composed the piece for harpsichord and named it *The Prince of Denmark's March.* Sir Henry Wood arranged the keyboard piece for trumpet, organ and drums, and mistakenly gave Purcell the credit for composing it. Now best known as a trumpet piece, this lively music often accompanies brides as they walk down the aisle.

A ballet tells a story through dance. Ballets first appeared in France in the 1700s and were accompanied by orchestral music that described each story's magical scenes. The Russian composer Pyotr Il'yich Tchaikovsky wrote music for several well-loved ballets, including *The Nutcracker.* His first ballet, *Swan Lake,* presents the story of a swan queen who falls in love with a prince. Tchaikovsky originally composed this ballet as an entertainment for his sister's children to dance. In 1876 he made it into a full professional production.

Air
from WATER MUSIC

George Frideric Handel (1685 – 1759)
Germany/England
Originally for chamber ensemble
Arranged by Fred Kern

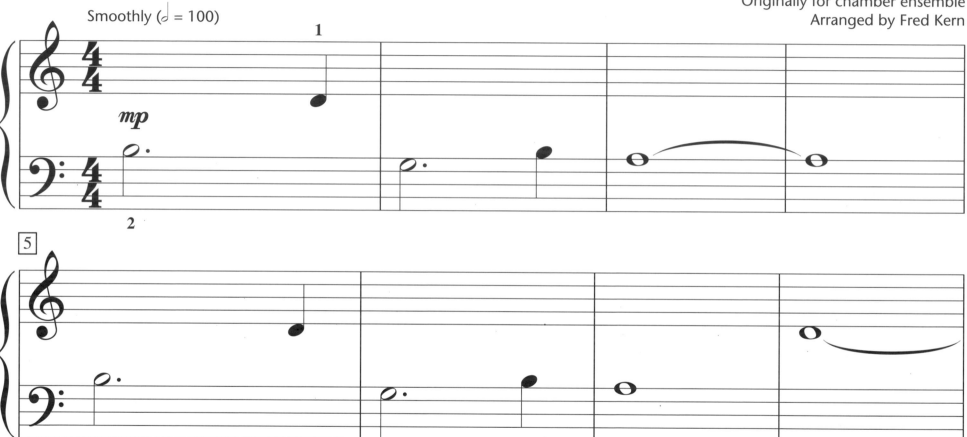

Accompaniment (Student plays one octave higher than written.)

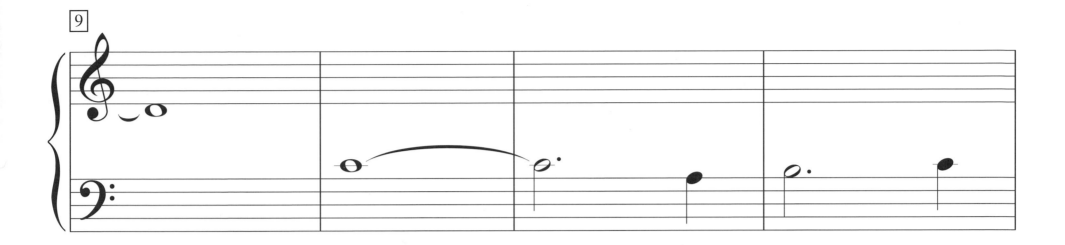

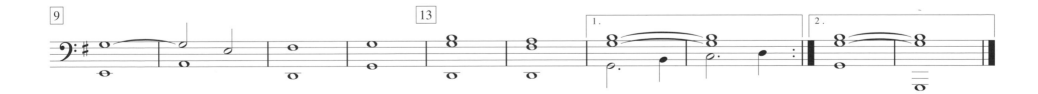

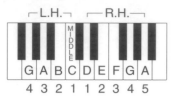

The Emperor Waltz

Johann Strauss, Jr. (1825 – 1899)
Austria
Originally for orchestra
Arranged by Phillip Keveren

Smoothly, Waltz tempo (♩ = 144)

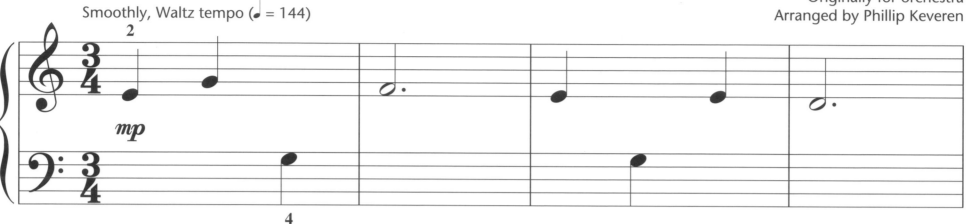

Accompaniment (Student plays one octave higher than written.)

Smoothly, Waltz tempo (♩ = 144)

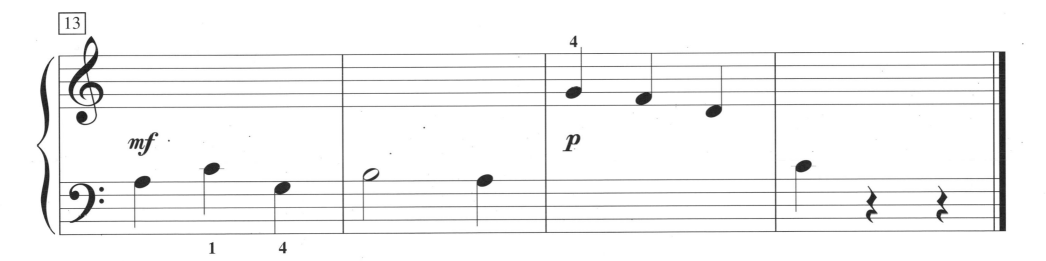

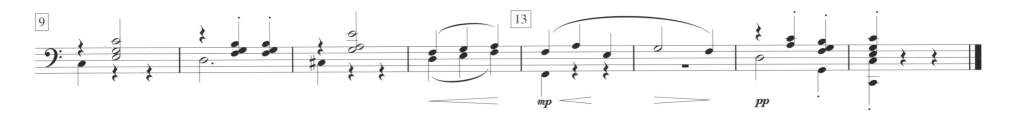

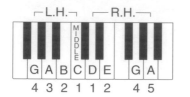

Morning
from PEER GYNT

Edvard Grieg (1843 – 1907)
Norway
Originally for orchestra
Arranged by Mona Rejino

Smoothly (♩ = 116)

Accompaniment (Student plays as written.)

Smoothly (♩ = 116)

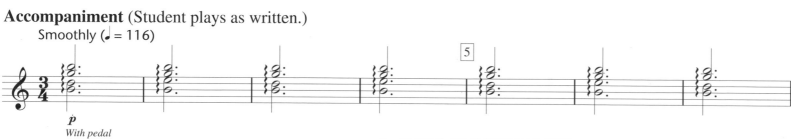

p

With pedal

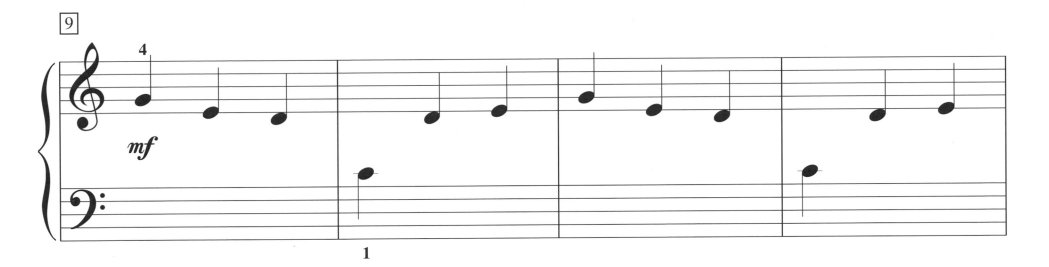

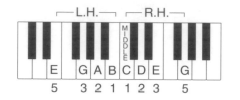

Russian Dance
"Trepak"
from the ballet THE NUTCRACKER

Pyotr Il'yich Tchaikovsky (1840 – 1893)
Russia
Originally for orchestra
Arranged by Fred Kern

Accompaniment (Student plays one octave higher than written.)

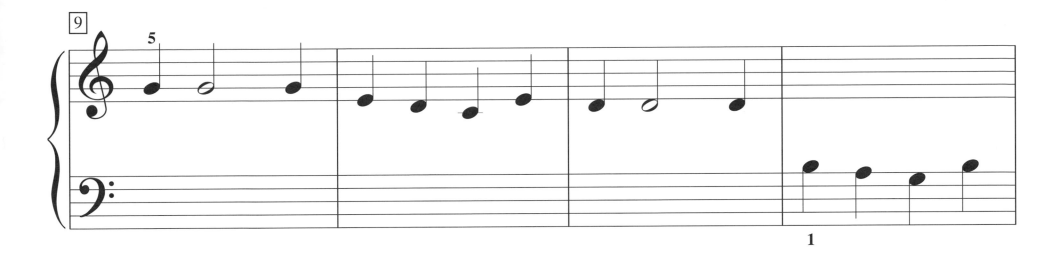

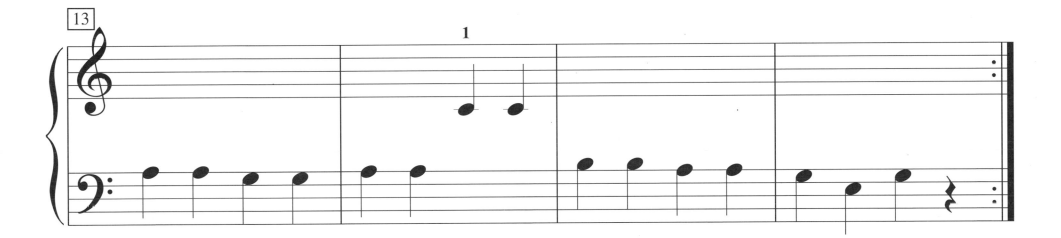

Symphony No. 3

"Eroica"
Fourth Movement Theme

Ludwig van Beethoven (1770 – 1827)
Germany/Austria
Originally for orchestra
Arranged by Mona Rejino

Accompaniment (Student plays one octave higher than written.)

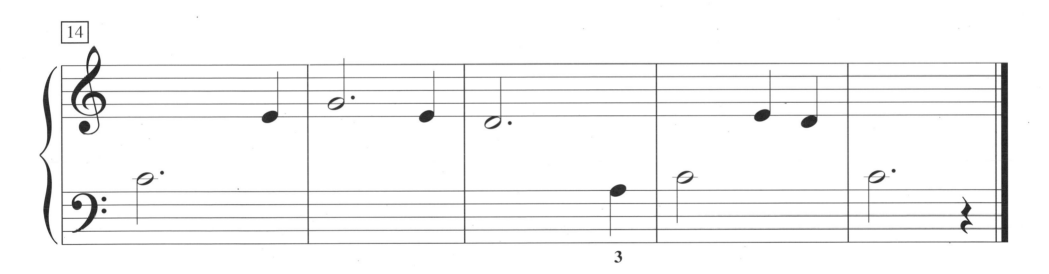

3

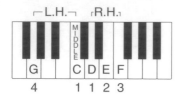

Trumpet Voluntary
(The Prince of Denmark's March)

Jeremiah Clarke (1674 – 1707)
England
Originally for harpsichord; later arranged for wind instruments
Arranged by Mona Rejino

Accompaniment (Student plays one octave higher than written.)

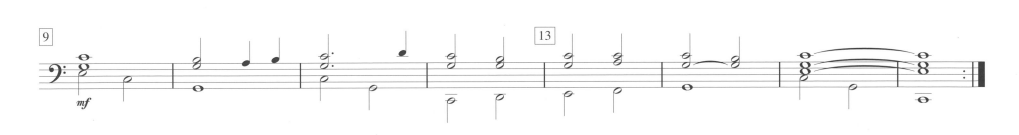

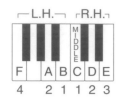

Theme
from the ballet SWAN LAKE

Pyotr Il'yich Tchaikovsky (1840 – 1893)
Russia
Originally for orchestra
Arranged by Fred Kern

Moderately (♩ = 152)

Accompaniment (Student plays one octave higher than written.)

Moderately (♩ = 152)

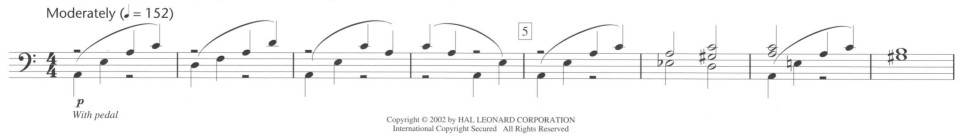

p
With pedal

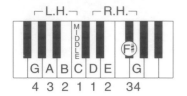

Can-Can
from the opera ORPHEUS IN THE UNDERWORLD

Jacques Offenbach (1819 – 1880)
France
Originally for chorus and orchestra
Arranged by Phillip Keveren

Accompaniment (Student plays one octave higher than written.)

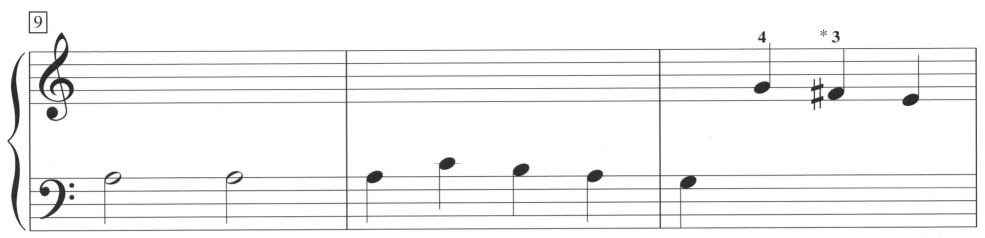

Sharp (♯): A sharp sign before a note means to play the next key to the right, either black or white.

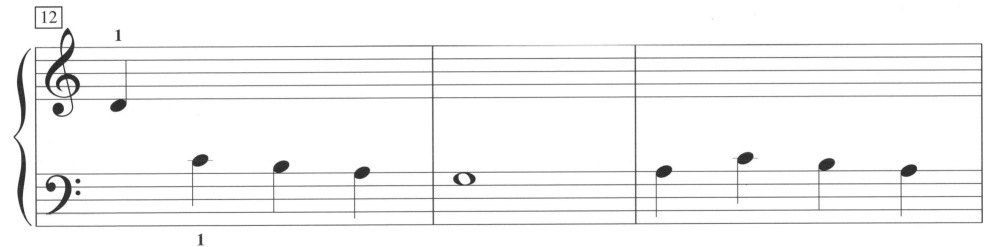

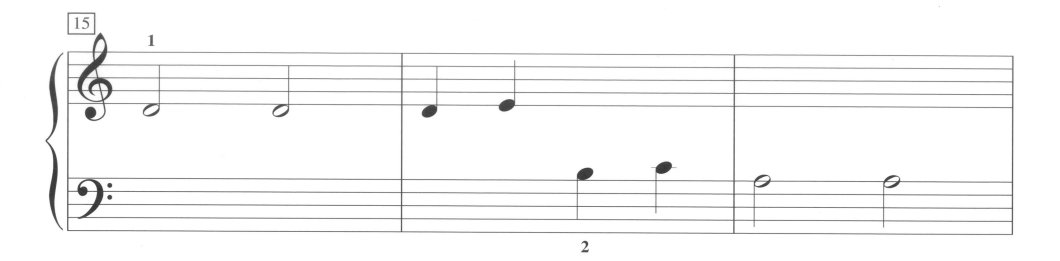

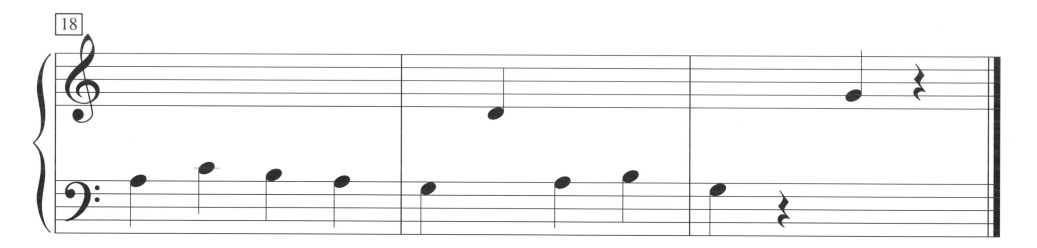

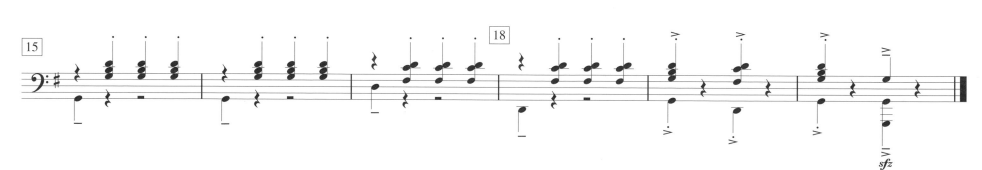

JOURNEY THROUGH THE
CLASSICS

COMPILED AND EDITED BY JENNIFER LINN

Journey Through the Classics is a four-volume piano repertoire series designed to lead students seamlessly from the easiest classics to the intermediate masterworks. The graded pieces are presented in a progressive order and feature a variety of classical favorites essential to any piano student's educational foundation. The authentic repertoire is ideal for auditions and recitals and each book includes a handy reference chart with the key, composer, stylistic period, and challenge elements listed for each piece. Quality and value make this series a perfect classical companion for any method.

BOOK 1 ELEMENTARY
00296870   Book Only.............................$5.99
00142808   Book/Online Audio..........$8.99

BOOK 2 LATE ELEMENTARY
00296871   Book Only.............................$5.99
00142809   Book/Online Audio..........$8.99

BOOK 3 EARLY INTERMEDIATE
00296872   Book Only.............................$5.99
00142810   Book/Online Audio..........$8.99

BOOK 4 INTERMEDIATE
00296873   Book Only.............................$6.99
00142811   Book/Online Audio..........$9.99

JOURNEY THROUGH
THE CLASSICS COMPLETE
(all 4 levels included in one book)
00110217   Book Only..................................$16.99
00123124   Book/2-CD Pack...........................$24.99

HAL•LEONARD® CORPORATION
7777 W. BLUEMOUND RD. P.O. BOX 13819 MILWAUKEE, WI 53213

See your local retailer or visit
www.halleonard.com

Prices, contents, and availability subject to change without notice.

0815

Hal Leonard Student Piano Library

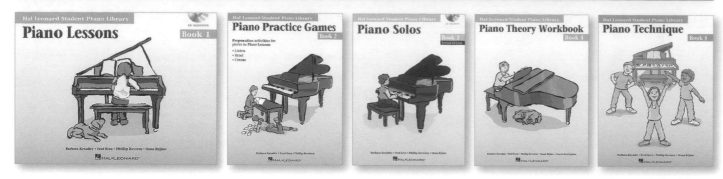

The Hal Leonard Student Piano Library has great music and solid pedagogy delivered in a truly creative and comprehensive method. It's that simple. A creative approach to learning using solid pedagogy and the best music produces skilled musicians! Great music means motivated students, inspired teachers and delighted parents. It's a method that encourages practice, progress, confidence, and best of all – success.

PIANO LESSONS BOOK 1
00296177 Book/Online Audio $8.99
00296001 Book Only $6.99

PIANO PRACTICE GAMES BOOK 1
00296002 .... $6.99

PIANO SOLOS BOOK 1
00296568 Book/Online Audio $8.99
00296003 Book Only $6.99

PIANO THEORY WORKBOOK BOOK 1
00296023 .... $6.99

PIANO TECHNIQUE BOOK 1
00296563 Book/Enhanced CD Pack $8.99
00296105 Book Only $6.99

NOTESPELLER FOR PIANO BOOK 1
00296088 .... $6.99

TEACHER'S GUIDE BOOK 1
00296048 .... $7.99

PIANO LESSONS BOOK 2
00296178 Book/Online Audio $8.99
00296006 Book Only $6.99

PIANO PRACTICE GAMES BOOK 2
00296007 .... $6.99

PIANO SOLOS BOOK 2
00296569 Book/Enhanced CD Pack $8.99
00296008 Book Only $6.99

PIANO THEORY WORKBOOK BOOK 2
00296024 .... $6.99

PIANO TECHNIQUE BOOK 2
00296564 Book/Enhanced CD Pack $8.99
00296106 Book Only $6.99

NOTESPELLER FOR PIANO BOOK 2
00296089 .... $6.99

TEACHER'S GUIDE BOOK 2
00296362 .... $6.95

PIANO LESSONS BOOK 3
00296179 Book/Online Audio $8.99
00296011 Book Only $6.99

PIANO PRACTICE GAMES BOOK 3
00296012 .... $6.99

PIANO SOLOS BOOK 3
00296570 Book/Enhanced CD Pack $8.99
00296013 Book Only $6.99

PIANO THEORY WORKBOOK BOOK 3
00296025 .... $6.99

PIANO TECHNIQUE BOOK 3
00296565 Book/Enhanced CD Pack $8.99
00296114 Book Only $6.99

NOTESPELLER FOR PIANO BOOK 3
00296167 .... $6.99

PIANO LESSONS BOOK 4
00296180 Book/Online Audio $8.99
00296026 Book Only $6.99

PIANO PRACTICE GAMES BOOK 4
00296027 .... $6.99

PIANO SOLOS BOOK 4
00296571 Book/Enhanced CD Pack $8.99
00296028 Book Only $6.99

PIANO THEORY WORKBOOK BOOK 4
00296038 .... $6.99

PIANO TECHNIQUE BOOK 4
00296566 Book/Enhanced CD Pack $8.99
00296115 Book Only $6.99

PIANO LESSONS BOOK 5
00296181 Book/Enhanced CD Pack $8.99
00296041 Book Only $6.99

PIANO SOLOS BOOK 5
00296572 Book/Enhanced CD Pack $8.99
00296043 Book Only $6.99

PIANO THEORY WORKBOOK BOOK 5
00296042 .... $6.99

PIANO TECHNIQUE BOOK 5
00296567 Book/Enhanced CD Pack $8.99
00296116 Book Only $6.99

ALL-IN-ONE PIANO LESSONS
00296761 Book A – Book/Online Audio $10.99
00296776 Book B – Book/Online Audio $10.99
00296851 Book C – Book/Online Audio $10.99
00296852 Book D – Book/Enhanced CD Pack $10.99

Prices, contents, and availability subject to change without notice.

HAL•LEONARD® CORPORATION
7777 W. BLUEMOUND RD. P.O. BOX 13819 MILWAUKEE, WI 53213

www.halleonard.com

1115